Table of Contents

I0021827

List of Figures

Introduction

This book is aimed for professionals working in any domain where knowledge of MS Excel is of utmost importance. Be it a fresher with MBA and a full time professionals working in any roles; this book will help them understand the different MS Excel features required in day to day excel operations. This book will deal on the basic concepts of MS Excel which an individual need to know before implementing them in their official activities. I have written this book not as a traditional text book where you only see the explanation of the individual topics. But tried to bring different scenarios we face in our daily office work to correlate the office requirement and MS Excel knowledge. You can find many unique topics such as Trendline, Spaklines, Trace Precedents, Trace Antecedents, Slicers and Timelines are covered in this book. I have included practice exercises at the end of each topics. This will help readers to judge their gathered knowledge.

For the esteemed reader of this book, I have compiled all the spreadsheet used to show examples in this book. Readers may like to drop their email to me for those samples at http://samratbiswass.blogspot.in/ . You are also open to use them in your day to day activities if it fits.

About Excel

Microsoft Excel is an example of a program called a "spreadsheet." Spreadsheets are used to organize real world data, such as a check register. Data can be numerical or alphanumeric. The key benefit to using a spreadsheet program is that you can make changes easily, including correcting spelling or values, adding, deleting, formatting, and relocating data. You can also program the spreadsheet to perform certain functions automatically and a spreadsheet can hold almost limitless amounts of data—a whole filing cabinet's worth of information can be included in a single spreadsheet. Once you create a spreadsheet, you can effortlessly print it, save it for later modifications. Microsoft Excel is a very powerful calculator—this course material is created using just a small number of its features as derived in the syllabus.

About Excel in MS Excel Series

The concept of this series cropped up in my mind while I was browsing internet and searching for different Excel reports. I came across many instances where I found in different forums users are willing to know more on excel usages in all domains. The requirement varies from basic level to middle level and then to the expert level. Although in the current market scenario there are many books which talks about MS Excel but none of them caters to the basic and advance requirement of features and capabilities. I realized that there are very few or no resources available in the current market to cater to the interested candidates who wants to know more on MS Excel particularly the available features and their usages. And there it pops in my mind that why not address a book to those fresher's who are willing to learn MS Excel and use its available feature in their day to day activities. So I conceived this book and meticulously planned the chapters after having interaction with many fresher, final year students willing to pursue their career where knowledge of Excel is on utmost importance. This book will cover the basic to expert level features on MS Excel with variety of examples. By going thru this, the reader of this book will not only know and understand how to work on the available features but will also able to correlate it with different reports applicable in daily operations.

Acknowledgement

I would like to say heartfelt thanks to my parents and my wife for the much needed encouragement while compiling this book. I would like to convey immense thanks to my childhood friend Mr. Bijay Mukherjee for helping me proof read the book content. He has completed the proof reading in a record time. Finally I would like to thank all the fresher and final year students who had encouraged me to bring the knowledge in the current form.

Disclaimer

While compiling this book I have taken numerous references from different portals and websites. Copyrights for any MS Excel features and objects used for references in this book are hold by the respective owners. Under no circumstances shall the author be liable for direct, indirect, special, incidental, or consequential damages resulting from the use, misuse, or inability to use the Excel features.

Chapter 1 | Know your Excel Ribbons

Conversation between Manager and Executive

Project Manager: Is this your first job?

Executive: Yes

Manager: Do you know the different tools in all the ribbons of MS Excel?

Executive: Not all!!

Manager: Read the following section and know more on Excel ribbons and available tools.

Home

Figure 1 Home Ribbon

Tools	Functions
Clipboard	Cut, Copy, Paste and Format Painter
Font	Font type, Size, color, Bold, Italics, Underline, Border, Fill Color
Alignment	Left, Right, Center, Orientation, Increase Decrease Indent, Wrap text, Merge and Center
Number	Number, Accounting number format, Increase Decrease Decimals
Styles	Conditional Formatting, Format as Table, Cell Styles
Cells	Insert, Delete and Format
Editing	AutoSum, Fill, Clear, Sort & Filter and Find & Select

Insert

Figure 2 Insert Ribbon

Tools	Functions
Tables	Insert and Recommended Pivot Table, Insert Table
Illustrations	Pictures, Online, Shapes, SmartArt, Screenshot
Apps	Apps for Office
Charts	Chart and Recommended charts, Pivot charts
Sparkline	Line, Column, Win/Loss
Filters	Slicers and Timelines
Links	Hyperlinks
Text	Text Box, Header & Footer, Word Wrap
Symbols	Equations and Symbols

Page Layout

Figure 3 Page Layout Ribbon

Tools	Functions
Themes	Themes, Colors, Fonts, Effects
Page Setup	Margin, Orientation, Size, Print Area, Page Breaks, Background and Print Titles
Scale to Fit	Width, Height, Scale
Sheet Options	Gridlines and Headings

Arrange	Bring to Forward, Send to Backward, Selection Pane and Align

Formulas

Figure 4 Formulas Ribbon

Tools	Functions
Function Library	Insert Functions, Financials, Logical, Text, Date & Time, Lookup & Reference, Math & Trigonometric Functions etc.
Defined Names	Name Manager, Define Name, Create from Selection
Formula Auditing	Trace Precedents, Trace Dependents, Remove Arrows, Show Formulas, Error Checking, Evaluate Formula, Watch Window
Calculations	Calculation Options
Solutions	Euro Conversion and Euro Formatting

Data

Figure 5 Data Ribbon

Tools	Functions
Get External Data	From Access, Web, Text and From Other Sources; Existing Connections

Connections	Refresh All, Connections, Properties and Edit Links
Sort and Filter	Sort, Filter and Advanced Filters
Data Tools	Text to Columns, Flash Fill, Remove Duplicates, Data Validations, Consolidate and What-If Analysis
Outline	Group, Ungroup and Subtotal

Review

Figure 6 Review Ribbon

Tools	Functions
Proofing	Spelling, Research and Thesaurus
Language	Translate
Comments	New Comments, Delete, Previous and Next button, Show all comments
Changes	Protect Sheet, Workbook and Share Workbook, Track Changes, Allow users to Edit Ranges

View

Figure 7 View Ribbon

Tools	Functions
Workbook Views	Normal, Page Break Preview, Page layout, Custom

	Views
Show	Ruler, Formula Bar, Gridlines and Headings
Zoom	Zoom, 100%, Zoom to Selection
Windows	New Window, Arrange All, Freeze Panes, Splits, Hide, View Side by Side, Synchronous Scrolling, Switch Windows
Macros	Creating Macros

Developer

Figure 8 Developer Ribbon

Tools	Functions
Code	Visual Basic, Macros, Record Macro, Use Relative References, Macro Security
Add-Ins	Add-Ins, COM Add-Ins
Controls	Insert, Design Mode, Properties, View Code, Run Dialog
XML	Source, Map Properties, Expansion Packs, Import
Modify	Document Panel

Chapter 2 | Cursor Shapes

Conversation between Manager and Executive

Executive: Why the cursor pointers are different all the time?

Manager: What!! Each cursor pointers define the mode of operation

Executive: How?

Manager: Read the following section.

In MS Excel we have seen that the cursor often changes its shape while using any available options. Each cursor pointers defines different mode of operations.

Cursor Shapes	When it appears?	What it does?
	This appears when you place your cursor over the Ribbon, Navigation and any other tools available in Excel	This helps to select menu and ribbon options
+	This appears when we put the cursor in the fill corner of the cell	This helps pull similar information in the subsequent cells
	This appears when you put the cursor over any graphic objects	This helps to hold the graphic and move from one place to another
	This appears when you put the cursor over a table column and rows	This allows user to select the column and rows at one go

I	This appears when you try to edit any content in the selected cell	This allows user to enter text in the cell
◄║►	This appears when you keep your cursor between rows and columns	This helps user to increase or decrease the width of columns and rows
↕ ↔ ↗ ↘	This appears when you would like to resize any graphic objects	Helps resizing the charts and graphics

Exercise 1

Practice all the Ribbon tools and its functions in the provided sheet. Get access of the practice sheet by providing your information and email id in http://samratbiswass.blogspot.in/

Chapter 3 | Data Sorting and Filter

Conversation between Manager and Executive

Manager: Sort the list of names on alphabetical order and share it with me.

Executive: Sort! But how?

Manager: Read the following section.

Executive: thanks

Sorting is a tool available under Home ribbon's Editing tool. Sorting a data helps you see it the way you want to see it. This also helps you find the value quickly. For example, you have list of 100 different names and they are not in an alphabetical order. So quickly searching a name from it would be very challenging, isn't it? To avoid this, you may like to quickly Sort the list of names in either 'A to Z' or 'Z to A' and quickly get the name which you want to have, following the alphabetical sequence.

Example: Suppose you have list of hundred names and surnames. Now you need to select a person from the list having the name starts with alphabet 'S'. If the name list is not sorted then it really very difficult to find that particular name without using the 'Find' option. So to sort the list of names you have to select the list or the list head and click right. In the temporary tool panel you will get the Sort option to sort alphabetically.

Find & Select

Find and Select is an option which allows you to search features like formulas, comments, conditional formatting, constants, and data validations in the given worksheet. These options are available in addition to the traditional options of Find, Replace, Go To and Go To Special.

Exercise 2

Practice all the Data Sorting and its related options in the provided data sheet. Get access of the practice sheet by providing your information and email id in http://samratbiswass.blogspot.in/

Chapter 4 | Data Validation

Conversation between Manager and Executive

Executive: Team members are filling data in irregular formatting

Manager: So you must have tough time create the report

Executive: Yes ☹

Manager: So why don't you use Data Validation to restrict your user for filling irregular data. Read the section below to know more on this…

Data validation in Excel helps you to restrict others to enter the value in the way you want them to enter. For example, you want that the user should only fill value from 1 to 100. If the user fills a value more than 100 then Data validation will restrict the user to fill the same. Simultaneously you can restrict user to update date as per the format you have decided. You can even allow "custom" in the data validation option by including some kind of formulas in it.

Figure 9 Data Validation 1

Types of Data Validation

Data validation has the following different 'Allow' options:-

1. Any Value – With this option you can allow all user to fill any value they like

2. Whole Number – You can allow user to input only Whole Number

3. Decimal- Users can only enter Decimal values in this options

4. List – You can allow user to choose from a provided list

5. Date – You can allow user to enter date as per the format you have defined; dd/mm/yy

6. Time – Time format can be defined; hh:mm:ss

7. Text – Allow user to provide text with some defined length say with not more than 10 letters

8. Custom – You can apply custom values in this options

Following different examples will help you to understand the above 'Data Validation' options in a better way.

Example: Whole Number

Say you want to restrict the user to fill the data *between** minimum 1 and maximum 20 in the given cell. Then with this option you can effectively restrict. In the data validation pop up the other two tabs are 'Input Message' and 'Error Alert'. You can provide a message to user on incorrect entry with a 'Style' symbol.

Figure 10 Data Validation 2

Example: Decimal

Similarly if you want to force the user to put only decimal values then you may like to use the Decimal Allow option.

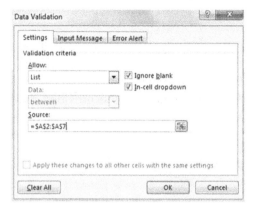

Figure 11 Data Validation 3

Example: List

List option is used when you want your users to enter the data from the list which you want. This options allows the user to choose only from the provided list. To create this drop down list, first you have to write the list in another or the same worksheet. Post that you have locate those range of cells in the 'Source' option. Once this validation is applied user will not able to enter any other values against the designated one. Here also we can put the 'Input Message' and 'Error Alert' for the user for entering incorrect entry. The output of the List data validation will be something as shown below.

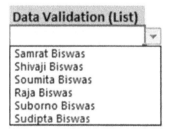

Figure 12 Data Validation 4

Same process is applicable for option Date, Time, and Text.

between, not between, equal to, not equal to, greater than, less than, greater than or equal to, less than equal to

Exercise 3

Practice all the Data Validation and its following options in the provided data sheet.

a.   Any Value
b.   Whole Number
c.   Decimal
d.   List
e.   Date
f.   Time
g.   Text
h.   Custom

Get access of the practice sheet by providing your information and email id in http://samratbiswass.blogspot.in/

Chapter 5 | Conditional Formatting

Conversation between Manager and Executive

Manager: Highlight the negative sales figure in Red. It should come automatically based on the conditions which we need.

Executive: But...how?

Manager: Read the section below to understand the usage of conditional formatting

In an excel data there may be few aspects, items and entries which you would like to highlight for your data presentation and here 'Conditional formatting' plays a very important role. Ideally it is one of the most important aspect of excel data presentation. This helps in easily spotting the trends, patters in your data by using bars, dot and icons for show casing highly important data.

Figure 13 Conditional Formatting 1

Creating Conditional Formatting

In the 'Home' ribbon we have an option available for 'Conditional Formatting' under 'Style' tool. In this there are multiple options to create Conditional formatting. Based on your need, requirement and better representation you may like to choose any of them.

Types of Conditional Formatting

Conditional Formatting are of following types:-

1. Highlight Cells
    a. Greater Than...
    b. Less Than...
    c. Between...
    d. Equals to...
    e. Text that Contains
    f. A Date Occurring...
    g. Duplicate Values...

2. Top/Bottom Rules
    a. Top 10 Items
    b. Top 10%
    c. Bottom 10 Items
    d. Bottom 10%
    e. Above Average
    f. Below Average

3. Data Bars
    a. Gradient Fill
    b. Solid Fill

4. Color Scales

5. Icon Sets
    a. Directional
    b. Shape – Like Traffic lights
    c. Indicators - Flags
    d. Rating – Harvey Balls

Exercise 4

Create the following conditional formatting in the table provided in the practice

sheet.

a.   Highlight Cells
b.   Top/Bottom Rules
c.   Data Bars
d.   Color Scales
e.   Icon Sets

Get access of the practice sheet by providing your information and email id in

http://samratbiswass.blogspot.in/

Chapter 6 | Excel Charts

Conversation between Manager and Executive

Manager: Please show me the monthly attrition and hiring rate in a line diagram?

Executive: I have those in a table, but not sure how to put that in a diagram.

Manager: Not an issue, go through the below explanation you will come to know.

Insert Charts

Charts are one of the important elements of data representations. Graphical chart help users to interpret the data quickly. MS Excel has different chart options like bars, column, bubble and doughnut etc.

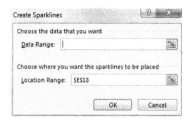

Figure 14 Insert Chart 1

Following are the different available charts in MS Excel:-

1. Column Chart

2. Bar Chart

3. Stock Surface or Radar Chart

4. Line Chart

5. Area Chart

6. Combo Chart

7. Pie or Doughnut Chart

8. Scatter or Bubble Chart

Figure 15 Insert Chart 2

Recommended Charts

Creating a chart with respect to the available data is completely on the user's choice and presentation skills. Sometime it may happen that whatever chart you are using has no clarity to the reader. To avoid this situation, MS Excel 2013 has provided an option of "Recommended Chart". If you select the data for which you want to create a chart then click this button; you will get a customized set of data which MS Excel thinks can be a best fit.

Illustrations

Illustrations tools in the Insert ribbon, provides an option for the user to insert picture from local, insert online pictures. It has the tool to create shapes to represent any flow diagram in the worksheet. Also provides the option of using SmartArt graphics for better representation of your data.

Figure 16 Illustrations

Sparkline

Sparklines are mini charts place in an individual cell representing an entire column of a data. This tool is available under Insert ribbon. There are three different types of Sparklines.

a) Line

b) Column

c) Win/ Loss

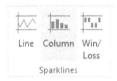

Figure 17 Sparklines 1

Example: Line Sparklines

Line Sparklines represent the range of values selected from the given table. Upon clicking the 'Line option, you get an option of 'Create Sparklines'. In this, you have to provide the 'Data Range' and the location where you want to get the Sparklines created. This helps create a line diagram based on the input value in a given cell.

Example: Column Sparklines

Name	Maths	Marks			Sparklines
		English	Computer	Hindi	
Samrat	56	80	75	81	
Shivaji	76	84	86	83	
Soumita	89	74	59	85	
Raja	86	86	82	64	
Suborno	77	84	77	72	
Sudipta	78	76	55	55	

Figure 18 Sparklines 2

For Column Sparklines, you have to select the 'Column' option in the Sparkline tool and provide the data range and location range. This option will help you create a column Sparklines in the given cell.

Example: Win/Loss Sparkline

Sometime it may happen that the values you have is both positive and negative. Generally it happens in winning and losing values in a sales cycle. In this case this Win/Loss Sparklines help user create a Sparklines having both positive and negative values in the diagram. Please refer to the below table for details.

Name	Deal Value in $
Phillips	560000
Braun	-100000
Videocon	230000
Samsung	-330000
Panasonic	450000
Salora	650000
Win/Loss Sparklines	

Figure 19 Sparklines 3

Editing the Sparkline Design

Figure 20 Sparklines Contextual Ribbon

When you create a Sparkline, the Contextual Tabs gets activated. It will provide you all the editing option of Sparkline design. For example, editing the source data, changing the type of Sparkline, style, colors, axis and how to show high points, low points etc.

Links Text or Hyperlink

This option helps you to put a hyperlink of any text and website in your document. This will also help you point out any other sections in your own document.

Symbols

In MS Excel, there is an option of inserting mathematical equations and different currency and copyright symbols. This tool is available in Insert Ribbon.

Exercise 5

1) Insert chart as per the table provided in the practice sheet.

a. Column Chart
b. Bar Chart
c. Stock Surface or Radar Chart
d. Line Chart
e. Area Chart
f. Combo Chart
g. Pie or Doughnut Chart
h. Scatter or Bubble Chart

2) Create Sparkline and edit them.

Get access of the practice sheet by providing your information and email id in http://samratbiswass.blogspot.in/

Chapter 7 | Page Layout

Figure 21 Page Layout Ribbon

Page Layout is another ribbon in MS Excel. As the name suggest this has all the tools which helps user setup their workbook or tab pages.

Themes

In the MS Excel 2013, you have got options to change your workbook theme. By default you get 'Office' as a theme. It has some defined colors, fonts and effects. There are around 24 different themes available in Excel. You may get more themes in the Microsoft Office website.

Page setup

As the name suggests, this option allows user to set up the page orientation. Be it a "Landscape" or "Portrait" you can choose the option which will get printed once you would like to take the print. Along with this this page setup options allows the user to adjust the scale and paper size. In the below shown pop out you can see that there other available options for setting up the page margin, headers and footer and Sheet details. All the given features under this option are used while taking the print of your excel sheet.

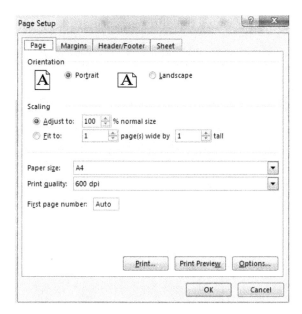

Figure 22 Page Setup Option

Custom Views

Conversation between Manager and Executive

Executive: Every time I have to rework on the formatting before I take a print for two different reports. And that is very time consuming. What to do?

Manager: Use Custom Views, it will allow you to save a specific formatting for the report which you take print daily.

Custom views save the current display and print settings that you can quickly apply in your spreadsheet before taking prints.

Step 1: Format the spreadsheet the way you want. And then click 'Custom View'. Assign and name to it and save it. You can use that custom view in future.

Likewise you can create multiple custom views for different formatting in the same worksheet.

Exercise 6

1) In your existing set of data change the le page layout. Make it landscape and apply header and footer into it.

2) Create a custom views and show case two different possibilities in your existing data set.

Get access of the practice sheet by providing your information and email id in http://samratbiswass.blogspot.in/

Chapter 8 | Auditing Worksheet

Trace Cells

Trace cells find that a selected cell is depended on which are other cells. This is applicable when the selected cell is having some formula. Precedent cells are cells that are referred to by a formula in another cell. For example, if cell D10 contains the formula =B5, cell B5 is a precedent to cell D10. Dependent cells contain formulas that refer to other cells. For example, if cell D10 contains the formula =B5, cell D10 is a dependent of cell B5.

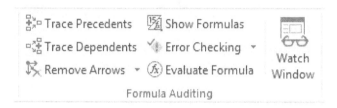

Figure 23 Formula Editing

The example given above is very simple. Either I can select cell C1 to see the cells/values used for getting the sum in the formula bar. Or else I can select and click F2 to see which cells are used to fetch this data.

Now imagine you have a big worksheet. In which you have numerous different formulas included in it. Some of the values are taken from Cell B1 and some from Z100 etc. By using the above two options it is sometime very difficult to know that from where you have taken the value for a specific formula. It is often very difficult to scroll and check. So unless you know from where your specific formula/cell has taken values, you may accidentally delete some value which will lead to errors like #N/A, #Value, and #DIV/0.

Here comes the use of Trace Precedents in Formula Ribbon's Formula Auditing tools.

Step 1: Select the cell in which you want to check the Precedents and then click "Trace Precedents". Clicking this tool will provide you all the cells from where the data is fetched and used in a formula.

Step 2: Similarly click "Trace Dependents" in the same cell, this will help you know other values in the sheet which are dependent on this value.

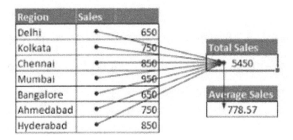

Figure 24 Trace Precedents and Antecedents

Watch and Evaluate Formulas

Evaluate Formula – is an option to learn how to evaluate your formulas in slow motion. It allows you to see the formula get calculated one step at a time. The command is under Tools - Formula Auditing - Evaluate Formula in Excel 2003 onwards, and on the Formulas ribbon in Excel 2007. Select a cell and choose Evaluate Formula. The dialog shows the formula. One term is underlined. This is the term that Excel will evaluate next. You can either evaluate that term or Step In.

Figure 25 Watch and Evaluate Formulas

Create a Data List Outline

Create a Data List outline is nothing but to create a set of columns with data in it. It helps to have a provision of adding date with the same format given to it. User can keep their cursor in the last cell and hit enter; this will create another row for entering data with same format. This saves enormous amount of time for post data entry formatting. To do this you need to get your table heading ready and visit 'Format as Table' option in your Home ribbon and select which table format you will like to use.

Date	Particulars	Amount

Figure 26 Data List Outline

Exercise 8

1) Create a data list outline with some define table headings. Use the select heading option in it.

2) Practice Trace Precedents and Trace Dependents

Get access of the practice sheet by providing your information and email id in http://samratbiswass.blogspot.in/

Chapter 9 | Pivot Tables

Pivot table is an interactive table that automatically extracts, organizes, and summarizes your data. We can use this to analyze the data, make comparisons, detect patterns and relationships and discover trends.

How to create a Pivot table

To create a pivot table first you have to select the entire table from which you want to have the pivot table. Post selecting the table you have to go to the Insert ribbon and click 'Pivot table'. This will pop out the 'Create Pivot Table' option seeking information like selecting the table range, location of the pivot table (new sheet or existing sheet). Once the selection is done click ok. This will create a new sheet (provided if you have selected new sheet as location). You will see a pivot table layout in the sheet and in the extreme right you will see the PivotTable Fields option activated. In the PivotTable Fields option, you can see all the field of your table from which you can select any or all of them as per your need. In the same PivotTable Fields option, you can see a quadrat below having cells like Filters, Columns, Rows and Values. Based on your requirement you can also pull the table fields in the respect cells. This will help you create your pivot table.

Figure 27 PivotTable Fields

Grouping Data containing Dates and Numbers

To group any data or dates you have select the table and go to the "Data ribbon". Here you have the option of grouping and ungrouping data.

Changing Scope of the Data Source

To change the Data Source of a pivot table, the user has to select the pivot table and click "Analyze" ribbon. In it there is an option of "Change Data Source". Post clicking this the user will get an option of "Change Pivot Table Data Source". In this you have to locate to the new dataset for which you want the Pivot table.

Inserting Calculated Fields

There are a few occasions where you need more information than your pivot table is designed to show, but it doesn't make sense to alter your source data to include this additional information. In these rare instances, it can be helpful to add a custom, calculated field to your pivot table. Custom fields can be set to display averages, percentages of a whole, variances or even a minimum or maximum value for the field.

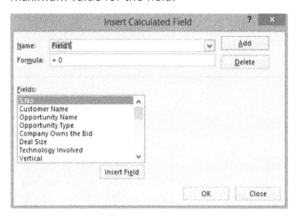

Figure 28 Insert Calculation Fields

Here's how to add custom fields in pivot tables so you can get the information you need with minimal effort.

Step 1: Select the first cell of the Pivot. Visit Analyze ribbon and Click "Fields, Items and Sets" options. From it select option "Calculated Fields"

Step 2: Insert Calculated Field option pops out. Name the calculated field you want to put. And write the formula to want to get a result. Click ok.

Changing Value Field Settings and Summarizing Values by Sum, Count, and Average etc.

This option allows user to get the desired output with respect to the numeric values available in the pivot table. For ex, you may need count of the certain entries or you may need sum, average of their values. To have the below option available, you have to first keep your cursor on top of the pivot table cell and then click right. This will lead you to have the "Field Settings" option. In the first tab of 'Subtotals & Filters', use the 'Custom' subtotal radio button to select if you want to have summation of the values or average or product.

Figure 29 Summarizing the Values

Formatting Pivot Table

From the same "Field Settings" dialog box you can have a tab 'Layout & Print'. This tab will help user to work out on the layout he is willing to have. These are used while you need to take print of the pivot table.

To have the below option available, you have to first keep your cursor on top of the pivot table cell and then click right. This will lead you to have the "Field Settings" option. In the second tab of 'Layout & Print', user can find multiple different options to work out on the pivot table layout.

Pivot Table Options

Pivot table options allows the user to work on naming the pivot table, its layout and format, tools and filters, display, printing and text. To get this option you first select the pivot table and then click right. You will get the option of "PivotTable Options". Select the option and you will get the below shown pop up.

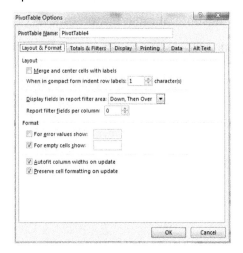

Figure 30 Pivot Table Options

Showing and Hiding the Grand Totals

Select the first cell of the pivot table in which you want to Show/Hide the Grand Totals. Click right you will get the option of opening Pivot Table Options. Once you click this option Pivot Table Option dialog box will pop in. Go to tab "Tools & Filters" and Check/uncheck the check box for Grand Totals.

Auto Refreshing Data in Pivot Table

You might have observed that every time you have to refresh your Pivot table post updating your master data from where you have created a Pivot table. To avoid this repetition, MS Excel has an option which helps the user to refresh the data every time you open the file. This forces the Pivot table to refresh it automatically while opening.

To perform this, select the pivot table and click right. Click "PivotTable Options" and visit the "Data" tab as shown below. There you will find the check box option of "Refresh data when opening file". Check the box given and save it. Next time round whenever you will open the sheet the pivot table will automatically get updated.

Figure 31 Pivot Table Auto Refreshing

Using Slicers and Timelines for Effective Filtering

Slicers provide buttons that you can click to filter PivotTable data. In addition to quick filtering, slicers also indicate the current filtering state, which makes it easy to understand what exactly is shown in a filtered PivotTable report.

Step 1: To get the Slicer option you have to go the "Insert" Ribbon's "Filter" tool. There you will have two options 1) Slicer and 2) Timelines.

Figure 32 Slicers

Step 2: Create you pivot table and then click Slicer. You will get the Slicer selection list.

Step 3: Select the Year and Margin or all three. You will get the slicer of your pivot table

Row Labels	Sum of Margin
2011	1.319
2012	1.319
2013	1.319
Grand Total	**3.957**

Figure 33 Slicer Result

Pivot Charts

Pivot chart option is available in the "Analyze" contextual ribbon. This only appears once the pivot table is created and selected. On clicking the Pivot Chart you will get an option of "Insert Chart". From this dialog box you can select the different types of chart available in MS Excel. Select the one which you like and click ok.

Exercise 9

1) Create a pivot table from your existing datasets. Use the value field settings sum and count option.

2) Use Pivot Table Option

3) Use Slicers and Timelines

Get access of the practice sheet by providing your information and email id in http://samratbiswass.blogspot.in/

Chapter 10 | Data Analysis

Create a Trend line

You can add a trend line or moving average to any data series in an unstacked, 2-D, area, bar, column, line, stock, xy (scatter), or bubble chart. A trend line is always associated with a data series, but it does not represent the data of that data series. Instead, it is used to depict trends in your existing data or forecasts of future data.

For example: Select the 2D graph and click right. You will get an option "Add Trend line". On clicking you will get the Add Trend line format option open. From there you can edit the formatting of the trend line.

Note: This can be only applicable in 2D graphs. In 3D graphs and pie charts "Add Trend line" option is not applicable.

Perform a What-if Analysis

Create Scenarios

We generally play around with different data figures in our spreadsheet. Sometime we need to create one report with some specific inputs whereas same time we need to see the same report with some different figures. Normally we update our data and then create report. And if changes required then we need to do it again. This really becomes cumbersome. To avoid this repetitive task MS Excel has one option called 'Scenario Manager' under tool What-if-analysis.

This helps user to create multiple scenarios with different data points and save it in your workbook. And whenever required you can show your scenarios and create different reports out of it.

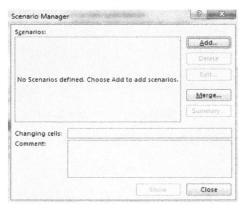

Figure 34 Scenario Manager

Steps to create Scenario:-

a. In the Scenario name box, type a name for the scenario.

b. In the Changing cells box, enter the references for the cells that you want to change. (Note: To preserve the original values for the changing cells, create a scenario that uses the original cell values before you create scenarios that change the values.)

c. Under Protection, select the options you want. Click OK.

d. In the Scenario Values dialog box, type the values you want for the changing cells.

e. To create the scenario, click OK.

f. If you want to create additional scenarios, click Add again, and then repeat the procedure. When you finish creating scenarios, click OK, and then click Close in the Scenario Manager Dialog box.

Goal Seek

If you know the result you want from a formula, but you aren't sure which input value the formula needs to get that result, use the Goal Seek feature.

For example, suppose you need to borrow money. You know how much money you want to borrow, how long you need to pay off the loan, and how much you can afford to pay each month. You can use Goal Seek to determine the interest rate you'll need to meet your loan goal.

Note   Goal Seek works only with one variable input value. If you want to work with more than one input value, such as a loan amount and a monthly payment, you use the Solver add-in.

Prepare the worksheet

1. Open a new, blank worksheet.

2. Add these labels in the first column to make it easier to read the worksheet.

   1. In cell A1, type Loan Amount.

   2. In cell A2, type Term in Months.

   3. In cell A3, type Interest Rate.

   4. In cell A4, type Payment.

	A	B
1	Loan Amount	100000
2	Terms in Month	180
3	Interest Rate	7%
4	Payment	($900.00)

Figure 35 Goal Seek

3. Add the known values.

>   1. In cell B1, type 100000. This is the amount that you want to borrow.

>   2. In cell B2, type 180. This is the number of months that you want to pay off the loan.

4. In cell B4, type =PMT (B3/12,B2,B1). The formula calculates the payment amount. In this example, you want to pay $900 each month. You don't enter that amount here, because you want to use Goal Seek to determine the interest rate, and Goal Seek requires that you start with a formula.

The formula refers to the values you entered in cells B1 and B2. The formula also refers to cell B3, which is where you'll have Goal Seek put the interest rate. The formula divides the value in B3 by 12 because you specified a monthly payment, and the PMT function assumes an annual interest rate.

Because cell B3 doesn't have a value, Excel assumes a 0% interest rate, and it returns a payment of $555.56. You can ignore that value for now. And for more information about the PMT function, see PMT function.

Use Goal Seek to determine the interest rate

1. On the Data tab, in the Data Tools group, click What-If Analysis, and then click Goal Seek.

2. In the Set cell box, enter B4, the cell with the formula you want to resolve.

3. In the To value box, type your payment amount,-900. The number is negative because it's a payment. This is the result you want the formula to return.

4. In the By changing cell box, enter B3, the reference to the cell that contains the value that you want to adjust. Remember the cell you enter here must be referenced by the formula you specify in the Set cell box.

5. Click OK.

Perform a Statistical Analysis with the Analysis ToolPak

If you need to develop complex statistical or engineering analyses, you can save steps and time by using the Analysis ToolPak. You provide the data and parameters for each analysis, and the tool uses the appropriate statistical or engineering macro functions to calculate and display the results in an output table. Some tools generate charts in addition to output tables.

The Analysis ToolPak includes the tools described below. To access these tools, click Data Analysis in the Analysis group on the Data tab. If the Data Analysis command is not available, you need to load the Analysis ToolPak add-in program.

How to install Analysis ToolPak?

Step 1: Go Excel Option. Visit "Add-Ins" and then select "Analysis ToolPak" in Active Application Add-ins and click go. You will get an option of "Add Ins". Click the check box of Analysis ToolPak. By doing this an Analysis tool bar will be reflected in your Excel Ribbon.

Descriptive Statistics

The Descriptive Statistics analysis tool generates a report of univariate statistics for data in the input range, providing information about the central tendency and variability of your data.

Histogram

The Histogram analysis tool calculates individual and cumulative frequencies for a cell range of data and data bins. This tool generates data for the number of occurrences of a value in a data set.

For example, in a class of 20 students, you can determine the distribution of scores in letter-grade categories. A histogram table presents the letter-grade boundaries and the number of scores between the lowest bound and the current bound. The single most-frequent score is the mode of the data.

Random Number Generation

The Random Number Generation analysis tool fills a range with independent random numbers that are drawn from one of several distributions. You can characterize the subjects in a population with a probability distribution. For example, you can use a normal distribution to characterize the population of individuals' heights, or you can use a Bernoulli distribution of two possible outcomes to characterize the population of coin-flip results.

Moving Average

The Moving Average analysis tool projects values in the forecast period, based on the average value of the variable over a specific number of preceding periods. A moving average provides trend information that a simple average of all historical data would mask.

Importing and Exporting Data

Export Excel Data

Conversation between Manager and Executive

Manager: Could you please convert the excel report in XML file? So that it can be updated in our SAP system.

Executive: How to do that?

Manager: Read the following section.

Step1: Click "FILE" ribbon and then visit "Export" Option. In the Option you will get two way to export excel data. Either you can create PDF or XPS document or you can change the file type into different file types available in this option.

Import a Delimited Text File

Conversation between Manager and Executive

Manager: Could you please port the text file we have received from delivery team into an excel sheet? I need to do an analysis out of it.

Executive: Shall I copy and paste it in a blank excel sheet?

Manager: No that is not the right way to do that. Why don't you read the following explanation to import a delimited text file!

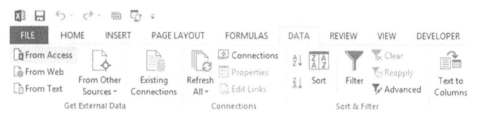

Figure 36 Data Ribbon

Step 1: To import a Delimited Text File, the user has to go to the "DATA" ribbon. In this there is a tool named "Get External Data". By the help of this tool user can import data from Access, Web or from Text files. The text file has to be delimited.

Step 2: Click "From Text" Option. An Import Text File dialog box will pop in. Locate the delimited file you want to import in excel. Click "Import".

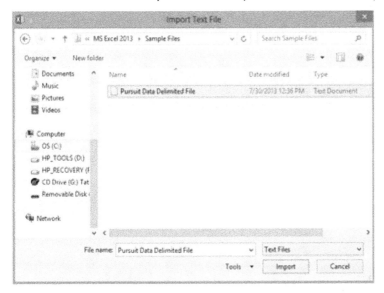

Figure 37 Import Text File 1

Post clicking "Import", you will get a "Text Import Wizard". It has 3 steps involved in it. Check My Data as headers and click Next.

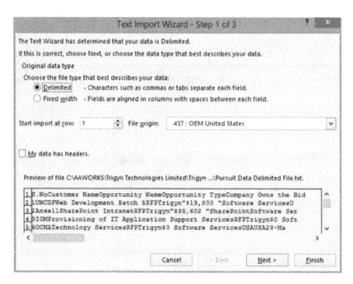

Figure 38 Text Import Wizard 1

Click the Delimiters available in your file. In the shown example it is "Tab" delimiter. Then click Next.

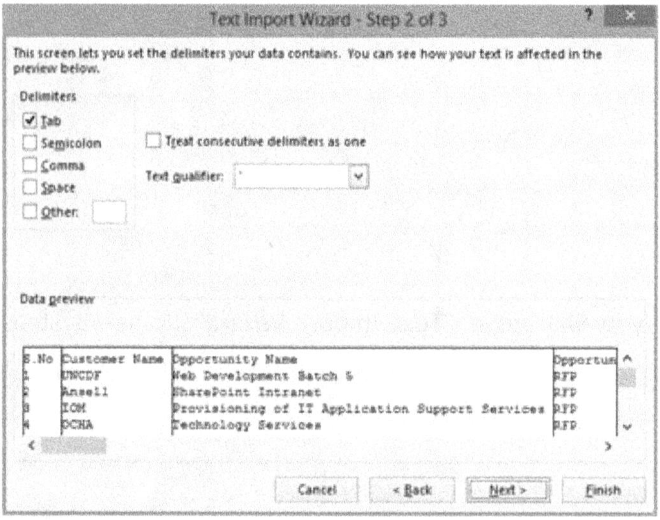

Figure 39 Text Import Wizard 2

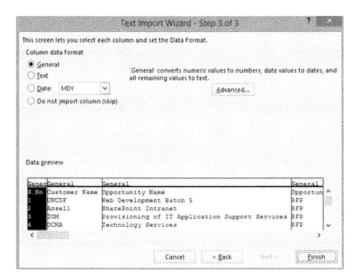

Figure 40 Text Import Wizard 3

Finally click Finish. This will pop the 'Import Data' menu for the location you want to put the data.

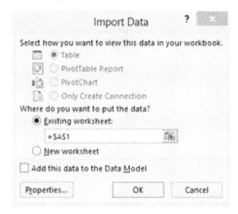

Figure 41 Import Data

Exercise 10

1) Create two scenario, one with the sales figure high by 15% and the other by 9% respectively.

Get access of the practice sheet by providing your information and email id in http://samratbiswass.blogspot.in/

Chapter 11 | Introduction to Macros

Microsoft Definition: A macro is a series of commands and functions that are stored in a Microsoft Visual Basic module and can be run whenever you need to perform the task.

Review and Purpose of Macros

Daily users of MS Excel often create a multiple reports of similar nature every day. They also use same repetitive commands every day which sometime become very troublesome. Users also need to provide daily report first thing in the morning to their bosses. So to avoid this repetitive steps, Excel has an option call Macros. These are basically Visual Basic codes recorded based on the movement and tools you click while creating the reports. To create and run a macro you do not need to be proficient in Visual Basic as such.

Displaying the Developer Ribbon

By default in MS Excel you do not get the Developer Ribbon loaded in your workbook. To load the Developer ribbon you need go to the File option and select Excel Option. As the name suggests this ribbon consists of Excel design, development and Macro tools.

Figure 42 Developer Ribbon

How to record a macro

Option for recording macro is available in the Data ribbon. Upon clicking the 'Record Macro' option from the code tool the 'Record Macro' dialog box pops up. This allows the user to name the macro and store in the respective workbook. If you want you can put the description of the macro in the given cell. This helps remembering the reason and purpose of recording the same.

How to create assign macros to buttons

Macros created by users can be used either visiting the Macro option and running the required macro code or it can be save in "Buttons" so that once you need you can just click the required Macro button and the macro will run and give the desired result.

To do user has to first open the Developer ribbon. In developer ribbon there is a tool called 'Control'. In control tool there is an option 'Insert'. After clicking the Insert command drop down symbol you will find the 'Form controls' and 'ActiveX controls'. From 'form controls' select the button option and create a button in your excel sheet. Once the button is created it will pop up a dialog box where you can link your existing macro and assign it with that the button.

Where to Save Macros

Macros can be saved in the same workbook, in a new workbook or the user can create a Personal Macro book as well for storing all his Macros. It is advisable to save the macro in the Personal Macro Book. Because this will help user to retrieve the recorded macro in any new files he wants to.

Figure 43 Save Macro

Absolute and relative record

Relative reference option is used to record the action related to the initial selected cell. If this option is selected before the macro recording then the recording will also pick the initial movement of your cursor. And every time you run the macro it will move it from one cell to another.

Running macros: Assigning to Quick Access Toolbar

To assign the macro in the quick access tool bar the user has to first go to the Excel Option. Then visit 'Quick Access Toolbar' and then select 'view macros'. Finally click Add to complete the process.

Exercise 11

1) Record a macro and run it. Check if is working the way you want.

2) Use the option Relative record and see the difference in the recording

3) Add Macro button in the quick access toolbar

Get access of the practice sheet by providing your information and email id in http://samratbiswass.blogspot.in/

Chapter 12 | MS Excel Sharing and Security

Sharing and security tools are available in Review ribbon.

Sharing a File

Scenario 1: Say you have a report in a spreadsheet. You want this report to be filled by others. Or in other words if you want to collaborate in this report and you may need to share it among the team members

Step 1: To share a file, click "REVIEW" ribbon and select option "Share Workbook".

Step 2: Select the user in the "Editing" tab whom you want to share this file. This is only possible if you are in a LAN.

Step 3: Select tab "Advanced" for different options such as "Track Changes", "Update Changes" etc. Finally click OK.

Tracking Changes

Conversation between Manager and Executive

Manager: In the shared file I want to see all the changes done by our team members. Could you please check if the track changes mode are on?

Executive: I can check this from previous data and find out what are the changes but it will become very time consuming. What to do?

Manager: For track changes please go through the below explanation you will come to know.

To activate the Track changes, please visit Review ribbon and click the option of track changes under Changes tool.

Step 1: To perform Track Changes a file, click "REVIEW" ribbon and select option "Track Changes" and then click "Highlight Changes. Then "Highlights Changes" dialogue box will pop up.

Figure 44 Review Ribbon

Step 2: Check "Track Changes" option and check the "When", "Who" options as well. Select "Where" if any particular location you want to track the changes. Finally click OK.

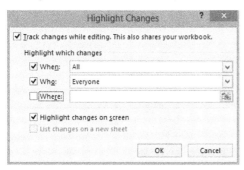

Figure 45 Highlight Changes

Accepting or Rejecting Changes

If the track changes are active then you can easily see the changes done in the sheet. This will not only show the current data but it will also show the pervious data in any given cell. You may like to accept and reject those changes.

Step 1: To perform Accepting and Rejecting Changes in a file, click "REVIEW" ribbon and select option "Track Changes" and then click "Accept/Reject Changes. If track changes mode was "On" in the current document then this option will be available for selection.

Inserting Comments

Sometime we may need to put comments on individual cell to provide any specific instruction to any of our team members. To do this we can use the option of "Inserting comments". This is available upon clicking right mouse button. We can also Show our given comments with a pop up box for better visibility. This can be done by using Show/Hide option available upon clicking right mouse button.

Protecting Cells, Sheets and Files

Option for protecting cells, sheets and files are available in the Review ribbon. Opting this will ask the user to put a password. Kindly note, the password has to be carefully stored. In case it is lost you may not be able to open the file anymore and cannot be retrieved either.

Figure 46 Protecting Cells, Sheets and Files

Workbook Structure

Microsoft Excel provides several layers for protecting your sheet and workbook. For example, you can protect your entire workbook, or you can protect a sheet and other elements in your sheet. Or you can protect your workbook structure from deliberate deleting or un-hiding your sheets by other users.

To prevent your workbook structure, you have two different options of doing this.

1) You can visit Review ribbon and click "Protect Workbook". This will open up a dialog box "Protect Structure and Windows". Select the "Structure" Checkbox and provide a password to lock your workbook structure. The password in this is optional but it is advisable to use a password to protect the structure.

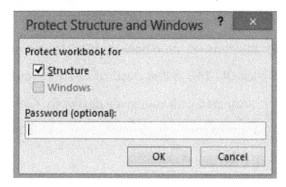

Figure 47 Protect Structure and Windows

2) You can visit FILE option and select the "Protect Workbook" option. This will further open up the same dialog box "Protect Structure and Windows". And rest you can follow the same instruction given above.

Protecting your workbook structure will not allow other users to deliberately delete, add or change the sheet in the workbook. In fact this will disable the "Right Click" features available to delete, add and move or copy, hide and unhide features.

Password Protecting a File

In MS Excel, there are two different ways of protecting your entire workbook. A) You can visit the "Protect Workbook" option and encrypt your spreadsheet with a password. B) Or you can visit the "Save As" option and protect your sheet.

A) Click the File tab and then click the "Protect Workbook" option as shown below. Put your password and click Ok. This will ask you to re-enter your password and that's it. Your file is protected with your given password. Keep it in mind that if you forget this password then it is somewhat impossible to retrieve it.

Figure 48 Protect Workbook Option

B) From this "Save As" option you cannot only protect the entire sheet but you can provide two different levels of protection in it. a) You can give a password to open the file b) You can give a separate file to modify the data.

This option helps you in the following case: You want to share the data with someone, but simultaneously you don't want the same user to modify the data. By the help of this level of protection you can restrict the user to only view the spreadsheet content.

Password Protecting a Cell Range

Step 1: To Protect a Workbook, click "REVIEW" tool bar and select option "Allow User to Edit Ranges". Give the range of cells which you want to protect and hit ok.

Figure 49 Range Password

Exercise 12

1) Practice protecting the cells, rows and files

Get access of the practice sheet by providing your information and email id in http://samratbiswass.blogspot.in/

Chapter 13 | Tool Descriptions

Quick Access Tool Bar

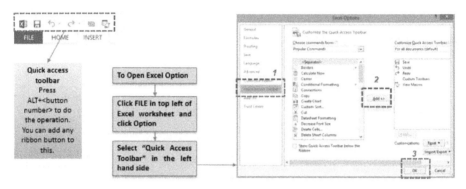

Figure 50 Quick Access Tool Bar

How to load Developer's ribbon in Excel 2013?

Developer's ribbon has tools like Code, Add-Inns, Controls, XML and Modify. This is used for creating and editing macros, inserting VB controls etc. By default this ribbon is not loaded by itself when you start your Excel. You have to check this option; to have this in your default ribbon.

How to do this?

After opening a blank excel spreadsheet, click File menu and then click Options. This will pop up the dialog box of Excel Options as shown below.

Visit Customize ribbon option in the left hand side and check the developers tab option in the main tab column in your right hand side. And then click Ok.

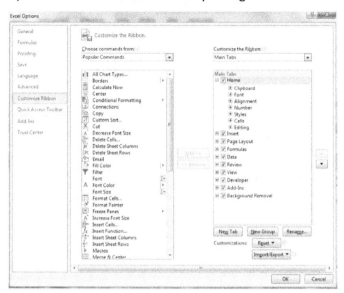

Figure 51 Excel Option

List of important key board shortcuts

In MS Excel there are huge list of short keys one can use. You can find many similar websites covering list of key board shortcuts. I tried to compile only few of them which are of regular use and can help you ease your work a bit.

Short Cuts	Usages
Alt	To see the use of shortcuts of all the available tools in Ribbon
F4	Repetition of the previous action
Alt+Enter	For putting a paragraph space inside a cell
Ctrl+1	Opens Format cell
Ctrl+T	Creates Table
Ctrl+5	This strike off the text
Alt+Ctrl+DD	For applying filter

References

1. MS Office 2013 https://support.office.com

2. Excel in MS Excel Blog - http://samratbiswass.blogspot.in/

3. Wikipedia

4. Wikihow

Upcoming Books

Excel in MS Excel for Bid and Proposal Management

This book will touch upon the usages of MS Excel in managing and bid and proposal. It will cover all the reports one has to maintain while on managing the pursuit effectively.

Bid Management – Process and Techniques

This will cover all the standard bid management process and techniques followed in the industry. This will help presales and Business development professionals to know the intricacies of bid management and effectively implement them in their pursuits to get positive outcomes.

MS Office Integration – Technique of Using Open Source Office automation applications

About the Author

 Samrat is an IT Presales Consultant, having 10 years of rich experience in MS Office. He has the experience of executing many Excel trainings covering many participants of various organization levels.

Currently he is associated with Capgemini as a Large Deal Bid Manager, IT Infrastructure Services and currently based out of Offenbach, Germany. Prior to Capgemini, he had worked for companies like Pitney Bowes, Cyient, and Microsoft. Samrat holds a PGD in International Business from SCDL, Pune and Applied GIS and Remote Sensing from Jadavpur University, Kolkata. He had obtained Microsoft Office Specialist (MOS) certification on advance MS Excel 2013. He also possesses' ITIL V3 foundation certification from APMG, GmbH.

Weekend Trainings for Corporate and Students

Considering the importance of Excel in day to day activities and its need for the fresher's and mid-level executives, I organize weekend programs to share knowledge on Excel at nominal fees for two days. Generally the weekend knowledge sharing sessions are held on the last Saturday and Sunday of the current month. Interested students and professionals can reach Excel in MS Excel thru the

Blog http://samratbiswass.blogspot.in/

Facebook Page https://www.facebook.com/Samrat.Biswas/

YouTube Channel https://www.youtube.com/watch?v=_1lyLbwRTS4

www.ingramcontent.com/pod-product-compliance
Lightning Source LLC
Chambersburg PA
CBHW070856070326
40690CB00009B/1865